KU-683-998

More of
The
World's Best
Doctor Jokes

More of
The
World's Best
Doctor Jokes

Dr Foster

ANGUS
& ROBERTSON
PUBLISHERS

ANGUS & ROBERTSON PUBLISHERS

Unit 4, Eden Park, 31 Waterloo Road,
North Ryde, NSW, Australia 2113, and
16 Golden Square, London W1R 4BN,
United Kingdom

This book is copyright.
Apart from any fair dealing for the
purposes of private study, research,
criticism or review, as permitted
under the Copyright Act, no part may
be reproduced by any process without
written permission. Inquiries should
be addressed to the publishers.

Illustrations and some of the text first
published by Hart Publishing Company Inc
First published in Australia
by Angus & Robertson Publishers in 1986
First published in the United Kingdom
by Angus & Robertson (UK) Ltd in 1986

Copyright© Angus & Robertson
Publishers, this compilation.

National Library of Australia
Cataloguing-in-publication data.

More of the world's best doctor jokes.
ISBN 0 207 15289 6.
1. Wit and humor. 2. Physicians —
Anecdotes, facetiae, satire, etc.
3. Medicine — Anecdotes, facetiae,
satire, etc.
808.88'2

Typeset in 12pt Goudy Old Style Bold
Printed in the United Kingdom

A famous Israeli pianist was giving a concert before a packed audience at London's Festival Hall. Right in the middle of the adagio movement of the Pathetique Sonata an elegant matron jumped to her feet.

"Is there a doctor in the house?" she cried.

"Yes madam," came the reply from several rows back, and a man got to his feet. "I'm a doctor," he said.

"Doctor!" beamed the matron, "have I got a girl for you!"

Young Mabel Smith went to see her doctor and complained of a frightful pain in the groin whenever she walked. She'd had it, she reported, for some weeks now and whenever she ventured out she was doubled up with agonising shooting pains. Of course she feared the worst. Could it be that she was pregnant?

The doctor asked Mabel to lie on the couch so that he could examine her. Mabel hoisted herself up painfully and lay waiting anxiously for the verdict.

"Ah ha," said the doctor with satisfaction. "Just hold still a minute and we'll have you out of trouble."

Suddenly Mabel heard a "snip, snip, snip".

"Good heavens!" she cried. "What are you doing?"

"All's well," came the reply. "I've just cut ten centimetres off the top of your boots."

"Doctor, are these pills habit forming?"
"Not if you take them regularly."

"Look, Mrs Brown," the doctor explained kindly, "it's natural that you and Mr Brown should feel less sexually active. After all he's eighty-seven and you're eighty-four, aren't you?"

"Yes, doctor," said the senior citizen. But it was obvious that she was still concerned.

"Well," said the doctor in an effort to reassure his patient, "tell me, when did you first notice that the urge was weakening?"

The old lady looked thoughtful, but there was nothing wrong with her memory.

"Well, there were a couple of times last night — and then again this morning," she explained.

"Doctor, I think I am beginning to lose my memory."
"When did you first notice that?"
"When did I first notice what?"

The nurse at the front desk answered the telephone. "Hello. Can I help you?"

"Yes, nurse, can you please tell me how Simon Masters is doing?"

"Just one moment," said the nurse. She pulled out Masters's chart and reread the doctor's notations. Then she answered, "He's doing very well. He should be out of here this coming Friday. Who's calling?"

"Simon Masters."

"Oh," said the nurse, "you're the patient!"

"Yes," he replied. "I can't seem to get any information about my condition from the doctor."

"Doctor, you must help me," the pretty young lady told the psychiatrist. "Every time a boy takes me out, I always end up saying 'yes'. And afterwards I feel guilty and depressed."

"I see," the analyst nodded. "And you want me to strengthen your resistance?"

"Certainly not!" exclaimed the distraught girl. "I want you to weaken my conscience!"

"Right, put your tongue out ... Good heavens, madam! Don't put that back in your mouth — you'll poison yourself!"

"If I take these pills will I get better?"
"Nobody I've given them to has ever come back."

Patrick's pregnant wife lived way out in the country and took ill one day shortly before her child was due. It was quite dark when the doctor arrived, and he asked, "Where is the little lady, Patrick?"

"She's over there in the barn where she collapsed."

With Patrick holding the lamp the doctor set about his job.

"Patrick, you're the proud father of a little boy."

Patrick said, "Doctor, we'll have a drink."

"Just a minute. Hold the light a little closer. You're the father of two."

"We'll open a bottle," said Patrick.

"Wait," the doctor said. "Hold the light a little closer. You're the father of three."

"And sure it's going to be a celebration and all," said Patrick.

"Just a minute," said the doctor. "Hold the light a little closer."

"I don't want to be difficult, doctor," said Patrick, "but do you think this bloody light's attracting them?"

An ageing and overweight businessman was going for a checkup for insurance purposes.

"Sex?" asked the doctor.

"Infrequently," the patient grunted.

"Is that one word or two?" the doctor inquired cautiously.

What is that which a flamingo can do with ease, a duck with difficulty, and a pigeon not at all?

And, moreover, what would you like to tell your doctor to do?

Take his bill and shove it up his . . .

Did you hear about the Irish doctor who stayed up nights trying to find a cure for insomnia?

"There's nothing wrong with you," said the psychiatrist to his patient. "Why, you're just as sane as I am!"

"But, doctor!" cried the patient, as he brushed wildly at himself, "it's these butterflies. They're all over me!"

"For heaven's sake!" cried the doctor, "don't brush them off on me!"

A venerable who had recently retired to a seaside town was suffering with a sore throat, and so paid his first visit to the local doctor.

"Well," the doctor reassured him, "you're in fine shape. But before you go, tell me something of your medical history."

"Sure, doc," smiled the ancient. "Well, I'd say that throughout my life my old-fellow has been a good barometer of my health and, though I say it myself, my health has generally been excellent.

"Why, as a teenager I was in great demand. There wasn't a weeknight went past but I had cause to exercise the old-fellow. And he was an enthusiast at his task, never flagging or failing. Why, every morning I'd wake and my organ would be so rock hard I couldn't push it down, even with two hands, to get my pants on.

"That continued, doc, throughout my life — every morning I had this tower that I just couldn't push down no matter how hard I tried."

"Remarkable," said the doctor. "And tell me, do you still have these morning erections?"

"I do, yes I do," said the old timer. "But do you know, doc, an extraordinary thing started to happen to me a few years ago. Suddenly I was able to push the old-fellow down with both hands. And in the last few weeks, I've done it with only one hand."

"Well, you must expect that kind of thing at your age," said the doctor.

"But I never expected anything of the kind!" objected the old timer. "Good heavens — what chap would imagine that at the age of eighty-four he'd start getting stronger?"

Then there was another elderly gent whose doctor suggested that he'd stay a lot fitter if he gave up half of his love life.

"Which half, doc?" asked the patient. "Thinking about it or talking about it?"

A seventy-five-year-old woman shuffled into Dr Meyerowitz's office. "Doctor," said told the physician, "I'm not feeling too good."

"I'm sorry, Mrs Kupnick, some things even modern medicine can't cure. I can't make you any younger, you know."

Mrs Kupnick replied, "Doctor, who asked you to make me younger? All I want is for you to make me older!"

Stuart Williams is sent to Dr Brown for psychological testing. Dr Brown gives him the Rorschach test. He shows Williams the first blot and asks him what he sees.

"A nude woman combing her hair."

He shows him the second ink blot and Williams says, "Oh, that's two people making love."

The third ink blot elicits, "That's two children playing doctor."

And so it goes . . .

"Well," says Dr Brown, "you certainly seem to have sex on your mind."

"What are you talking about, doc! You're the one who's showing me all those dirty pictures."

"Doc, please tell me the truth, I can take it. Are you expecting any complications? I just heard that a man who was being treated for jaundice died last night of diphtheria."

"Don't be silly," responded the eminent physician. "You've got nothing to worry about. If I'm treating you for jaundice, you'll die of jaundice!"

One day the powerful witchdoctor of the Umuluyen tribe who lived near the great Zambezi River was visited by a troubled old lion seeking help. The old lion explained that his shaggy mane had become the home for a flock of birds, and as everyone knows, little birds in their nests don't agree. It was the chirping and squabbling all night long that troubled the old jungle king. He could no longer sleep, and was losing his energy.

The witchdoctor listened to his tale of woe, then told him the solution was simple. All he had to do was to rub yeast in his underwear and the birds would go.

The old lion ambled off and tried this cure. Miraculously it worked, and so he returned to the witchdoctor to thank him and pay his fee.

"Forget the fee," said the witchdoctor. "It was a pleasure to help the king of the jungle."

"But all that specialised knowledge! Surely you need recompense for all your years of study," the lion said.

"Special knowledge, my eye," said the witchdoctor. "Everyone knows that yeast is yeast and vest is vest and never the mane shall tweet!"

Two specialists visited the funeral home to pay their last respects to a life-long patient.

"He looks pretty good, doesn't he?" remarked one.

"So he should," replied the other. "He just got out of the hospital!"

As the surgeon was making his hospital round he was stopped by the pretty young thing in bed 12. He had operated on her several days before.

"Doctor, do you think the scars will show?" she asked.

"That will be entirely up to you," he replied.

Mrs Albert goes to consult a psychiatrist. After the initial greetings, the doctor says kindly, "Well, what seems to be the problem?"

"Well," says Mrs Albert, "where should I begin — with my childhood or my adultery?"

"You'll have to help me, doctor. It's my husband. He's at me all the time. Before breakfast, after breakfast, again at lunchtime, then before tea, and after tea until we go to bed, then all night long. Why, the other day I was bending over getting some food out of the freezer when up he came and we're at it again."

"Perhaps he's only trying to show you how much he loves you," the doctor volunteered.

"You're kidding!" she replied. "In the supermarket?"

A young man went along to see his doctor with a strange complaint.

"Doc, every day I get up and get dressed and suddenly I get an intense headache and that's accompanied by the sound of bells ringing in my ears. I've tried all kinds of pain-killers but nothing helps. What's wrong with me?"

The doctor gave him a thorough checkup but he could find no obvious cause of the painful affliction. Worried, he referred the young man to an ear, nose and throat specialist.

After hearing the story about the intense headache which was always accompanied by the sound of bells ringing, the specialist decided to operate. The operation was a lengthy affair involving the removal of two nerve endings at the base of the skull. As our hero left the hospital, days later, he found he was slightly deaf in one ear and had a permanent list to the left. He also had an intense headache and the sound of bells ringing in his ear.

Well, for several months he put up with the pain and the noise until finally he could endure it no longer. He went back to his doctor to see if there were any new miracles of medical science that could bring relief.

Sadly the doctor shook his head. The young man's case had troubled him from the start because he believed there was only one cure and that was a drastic one — castration.

"Anything," cried the young man. "Anything to stop the intense headache and ringing bells."

Several weeks after the operation the patient was released from hospital and decided to cheer himself up with some new clothes.

"What size does sir take?" asked the assistant hovering over the trays of underpants.

"Well, I used to take size 12 but I'm not sure any more," the young man said in some embarrassment.

"Size 12 sir! Oh no, sir. You'd need a size 14 at least sir," came the reply. "Why, sir, if you wore size 12 you'd find you had an intense headache and the sound of bells ringing in your ears."

Midshipman Able returned from an eleven-month stint at sea to find that his wife was about to have a baby.

"Listen, Ruby," he said, "I can count as well as any man and you can't tell me that that baby will be mine."

But Ruby denied any affair with another man. So Able consulted his doctor as to the possibility of it being his.

"Ah ha," the doctor replied, "in our profession this is what's called a grudge pregnancy — someone's had it in for you."

He was the most haggard-looking patient the doctor had seen in a very long time.

"I can't sleep," he moaned, tearing at his thinning hair. "I've got dogs to the left of me, dogs to the right of me, dogs all round me and they bark all night. I tell you, they're driving me mad."

"There's a new sleeping pill on the market called Sleepamatic," cooed the doctor sympathetically. "I'm having fabulous success with it."

The patient staggered home from the chemist with the pills clutched tightly in his hand. A week later, he was back in the doctor's surgery, looking even worse than before.

"It's no good," he groaned, "I haven't slept for a week. I'm up all night chasing those damn dogs, and even when I manage to catch them, they won't swallow the pills."

Patient to psychiatrist: "Nobody talks to me."
Psychiatrist: "Next!"

A woman walked into the surgeon's office, dragging her son behind her. "Mister, I just want to ask you one question. Can a boy of thirteen take out his own appendix?"

"Most certainly not, madam!" the surgeon replied.

She belted her son on the ear and said, "Didn't I tell you, Sidney? Now put it back at once!"

A very, very eminent surgeon dies. When he gets to heaven, he finds himself in this tremendously long queue. He's not used to waiting, so he barges up to the front, and says to St Peter, "Do you know who I am? I'm Dr Mortimer, the famous brain surgeon."

"Sorry," St Peter says. "Up here everyone is the same. You'll have to wait in line along with all the others."

Fuming, Dr Mortimer walks back to the end of the queue. He stands there impatiently, shuffling from one foot to the other. Suddenly a little guy in a doctor's outfit comes in and walks right up to St Peter. St Peter waves him right in.

Dr Mortimer rushes back up to St Peter, and shrieks, "What's with you? This is an unknown little intern here, and I am a famous brain surgeon, and you told me to queue, but you let him in."

"Take it easy," says St Peter, "you've got it wrong — that's not an unknown little intern. That was God. He likes to play doctor."

The apprentice had been left in charge of the chemist's shop during the lunch-hour, and when the chemist returned, he asked if there had been any customers.

"Just one," said the apprentice, "a fellow with a hacking cough, so I gave him a dose of castor oil."

"You *what?*" demanded the chemist. "Castor oil isn't a remedy for a cough!"

The apprentice looked puzzled. "Well, it seems to have worked," he said. "That's him over there hanging on to that lamp-post, and he hasn't dared cough in over half an hour!"

Two young Indian doctors were conversing while doing the rounds of the maternity ward of a London hospital.

"You know, Rachid," said one, "I'm sure you'll find it's spelt W.H.O.M.B.E."

"No, no, Kahlil, you are wrong," said Rachid. "It's spelt W.O.O.M.B.H. to be sure."

The ward sister who had overheard their conversation felt it her duty to comment.

"Doctors," she said, "forgive the intrusion, but you'll find it's spelt W.O.M.B.," and she went off about her duties.

As she disappeared from sight Rachid turned to Kahlil. "Silly old trout she is eh? Bet she's never seen a water buffalo, let alone heard one fart underwater."

"Well, doctor," asked the applicant for a life insurance policy, "how do I stand?"

"Darned if I know," admitted the doctor. "It's a miracle!"

A young and newly accredited G.P. was looking over the practice that was for sale in a remote region of the Scottish Highlands. The young man could not help but be impressed by the look of the proposition. There was a comfortable house, office and lab, a barn and a garden well stocked with fruit and vegetables.

The old doctor who was showing him round explained that he was retiring, so that everything was included in the very reasonable price.

The young doctor was intrigued. "How," he wondered aloud, "has all this been accomplished in a small community with a scattered population and no great signs of wealth?"

"Thrift, laddie, simple thrift and attention to wee details," the old doctor said, and went on to give an example.

"Now in summertime all the folk round here take themselves off on holidays — mostly to the big city. One or two weeks later back they come tired out and looking peaky. The wife and I, we stay at home but on really lovely days we go out for a picnic and gather herbs.

"In the autumn, we have to have the fire lit in the kitchen stove anyway, so it doesn't cost us an extra penny to put those herbs in a pot and brew up a good old-fashioned tonic. We get out all the bottles we've been saving, sterilise them and bottle up the tonic. It hasn't cost us a penny.

"Now when the spring comes everyone's out and about again. You can't help seeing your patients wherever you go. Whenever I run into one I'll say, 'Well Mrs . . . you don't look so well. What's the matter?'

" 'Doctor,' she'll complain, 'it's the spring

cleaning. I'm so run down I don't know that I'll be able to finish it!'

" 'Lassie,' I'll say, 'what you need is some good old-fashioned spring tonic. Call and get some anytime. 'Tis very inexpensive.'

"Well, I charge them £1.50p per bottle. Not a fortune you'll agree, but laddie, it's all clear profit.

"Then maybe a month, or maybe two, later I'll see Mrs . . . again and I'll say, 'Lassie, you are looking better,' and she'll agree that the tonic has been effective.

" 'Now, lassie,' I'll say, 'this is just the time of life when you ought to come around for a physical checkup. At your time of life we expect the changes you know, so we'd best make an appointment right now. And by the way, when you come be sure to bring a specimen.'

"And that, laddie, is how we always get our bottles back."

"I've been in that waiting-room of yours so long, doc," the well-known malingerer complained, "I've caught three more diseases. I tell you what I need," he said. "I need something to make me sweat."

So the doctor certified him fit.

There seemed to be nothing he could do for the young man, so the G.P. contacted the psychiatrist who worked in the same building and asked him to call on the man as soon as possible.

"He seems to be wasting away, and damned if I can find the reason for it," the G.P. said.

The psychiatrist agreed to call that very afternoon. Several hours later he reported back to the worried G.P. "Well, the diagnosis is easy — he's simply suffering from chronic fatigue caused by over-involvement in local politics."

"That's amazing," the G.P. gasped. "You were only gone a short while; how did you come to diagnose that so quickly?"

"Easy," replied the psychiatrist. "When I was taking his temperature I accidentally dropped the thermometer and when I bent down to pick it up I saw the lady mayor under the bed."

Three young medical students were discussing the theory of pre-natal influence.

"It's obviously an absurd theory," scoffed one. "It's been disproved every time it's investigated. For example, before I was born, my mother broke a huge pile of LP records. But it's never bothered me ... bothered me ... bothered me."

A man and his wife had a serious problem. The man was incontinent and no matter how little he had to drink before bed-time, he was forced to visit the bathroom many times during the night. He tried all kinds of remedies without success until one night his wife, who was getting little sleep, took things into her own hands and with a length of blue ribbon she found in her sewing basket, tied off the root of the problem.

Next morning her husband came to breakfast elated. "You look pleased with yourself," the wife observed.

"And so I should," said the husband, proudly. "I don't know where I got to last night, but I tell you something ... I won first prize!"

Mr Carson placed a frantic phone call to his doctor and explained that his wife, who always slept with her mouth open, had a mouse caught in her throat.

"I'll be over in a few minutes," said the doctor. "In the meantime, try waving a piece of cheese in front of her mouth."

When the doctor reached the Carson apartment, he found Mr Carson waving a large haddock in front of his wife's face.

"What are you doing?" exclaimed the doctor. "I told you to wave cheese. Mice don't like haddock."

"I know," Mr Carson gasped, "but I've got to get the cat out first."

An agitated woman walked into a public hospital.

"What can I do for you?" a receptionist asked, politely.

"I want to see an upturn," the woman said.

"You mean an intern?"

"Well — I want a contamination."

"You mean an examination."

"Anyhow, I want to go to the fraternity ward."

"You mean maternity ward."

At that the woman did her block. "Upturn, intern, contamination, examination, fraternity, maternity — what the hell! All I know is that I haven't demonstrated this month and there's something wrong with me Ovaltines. I think I'm stagnant!"

A man walked into a psychiatrist's office and stuffed tobacco into his right ear.

"Well, it's obvious that you need me," said the doctor.

"I sure do," the man agreed. "Got a match?"

A man walked into his doctor's office with a banana stuck in each ear.

"Listen, Ned," said the doctor. "What's the idea of a banana in each ear?"

"Sorry, doc, I can't hear you," said Ned. "I've got a banana in each ear."

"Well, dear," asked the psychiatrist of his young lady patient, "what did you dream last night?"

"I didn't dream last night, doctor, I had a marvellously peaceful night's sleep."

"Never mind about 'peaceful'," said the doctor. "How am I supposed to help you if you won't do your homework?"

Mrs Casey accompanied her daughter Kathleen to her appointment with Dr Flynn and explained the situation.

"Sure, she's been having some strange symptoms and it's worried about her I am."

Dr Flynn examined Kathleen carefully, then announced, "Sure, it's pregnant your daughter is."

"Saints preserve us," gasped Mrs Casey. "Will you be listening to the great spalpeen. My daughter pregnant! I've never heard such nonsense, indeed I haven't," and she turned confidently to Kathleen for confirmation.

Kathleen blushed and replied with every vestige of great modesty, "No, no, of course not. Why, I've never even kissed a man!"

Flynn looked from mother to daughter and back again. Then, silently, he stood up and walked to the window. He stared out and continued to stare with apparently great concentration.

Finally Mrs Casey could stand it no longer and was compelled to ask, "Doctor, is there something wrong out there?"

"No," said Flynn. "Sure, it's just that the last time anything like this happened, a star appeared in the East and I was looking to see if another one was going to show up at all."

Mrs Hallaway was stunned to see her psychiatrist running down the street with a couch on his back.

"Doctor Stone!" she cried. "What are you doing?"

"Making house calls!" came back the reply.

"Doctor," a man confessed to his psychiatrist, "I'm afraid that I'm in love with a horse."

"Is it male or female?" the doctor asked.

"Female, of course," the man snapped back. "What do you think I am, a queer?"

"I'm rather embarrassed about this," confided a patient to his doctor, "but I'm having trouble with my love life at home."

"Well, Norm, there's nothing to worry about — all you need to do to get you going is to take off 10 kilos and run about 10 kilometres a day for two weeks," the doctor advised.

It was two weeks later that Norm called the doctor. "Well doc, I took off 10 kilos and I've been running 10 kilometres a day."

"So, how is your love life now?"

"Hell knows, I'm 140 kilometres away!"

A wide-eyed character who was convinced he was Napoleon burst into a psychiatrist's office, thrust his hand inside his coat, and declared, "It isn't myself I've come to see you about, doctor. It's my wife, Josephine. She thinks she's Mrs Richardson."

Mr Gerald came round in a three-bed hospital ward after his operation.

"Thank goodness that's over," he said to his room-mates.

"Don't speak too soon," said one. "They left a swab in me."

"Good heavens," cried Gerald.

"That's nothing," said the second, "they left a scalpel in me!"

"How terrible!"

Just at that moment the door opened and in came the surgeon.

"Good afternoon gentlemen!" he said breezily. "Has anyone seen my briefcase?"

Gerald fainted . . .

As the doctor left his crowded office to go out and move his car, he reassured his patients. "Don't anybody get better, I'll be right back."

"Oh, oh," wailed a lady patient. "What I'd give for just one good night's sleep."

"Try taking a glass of warm milk and eating an apple just before you retire," suggested the doctor.

"But, doctor," protested his patient. "Six months ago you told me not to eat a bite for three hours before going to bed."

"I know, my dear lady," bubbled the doctor, "but you have no idea what tremendous strides medical science has registered in that period."

Maurice forgot to tell his wife Florrie that he'd lacquered the toilet seat, with the inevitable result — Florrie and the throne became as one, inseparable.

Maurice, acting swiftly before panic could set in, severed the seat from the pedestal and, tucking his wife's dress neatly over the offence, escorted her to the local G.P. There he rushed her past waiting patients and into the consulting room, where he bared her all for the doctor's inspection.

"Yes, very attractive," the bemused doctor admitted. "But why did you have it framed?"

Overheard on a bus: "My doctor says I must give up those little intimate dinners for two unless I have someone eating with me."

Tony saw Joe rushing down the street. He grabbed Joe's arm and said, "Hi, feller, I —"

Before he could go any further, Joe interrupted, "Listen, I'm in a great hurry. I don't have time to talk to you now."

"I just wanted to ask you one question. What's your big rush anyway?"

"I have a session with my psychiatrist and I'm a little late already."

"So what, so you'll be a little late."

"No, that's impossible. He starts whether I'm there or not."

"You'll see, Bob, you'll soon wonder why you ever wanted a boy," the doctor consoled the new father of a baby girl.

"Oh, it's all right," the father assured him. "If I couldn't have a boy, my second choice was a girl."

The new assistant was eager to learn the marriage guidance officer's technique. So he sat quietly in his office and listened while the counsellor interviewed each spouse separately.

Mr Neilson listened patiently to the wife's side of the story, only interrupting occasionally to murmur "Ah ha" or "I see". When she was finished he leant over, took her hands in his, and, patting them gently said, "You are so right. You are so right."

After the wife left, the husband entered and gave his side of the story. The counsellor made the same encouraging interjections, and when the husband got up to leave, he patted him on the shoulder and sighed, "You are so right. You are so right."

The assistant was nonplussed, and as soon as the couple had left he approached his boss and asked: "How can you tell the wife she was right and then tell the husband he was right? They both can't be right!"

"You are so right. You are so right," Mr Neilson muttered.

"Martha, someone's just told me about Fred — I hear he was in plaster. What happened?" a neighbour asked sympathetically of the distraught wife.

"It's his knee," replied Martha. "I found a blonde on it."

Golda Meir was asked, "How was Israel able to win the 1967 war in only six days?"

She answered, "Well, you know, in Israel we don't have a permanent professional army. Our soldiers are civilians. And you know in Israel we have a lot of doctors, dentists and psychiatrists. So, when there's a war, we call them up and we put them in the front line, and we call out, 'Charge!' And boy! Do they know how to charge!"

"Say aah," the doctor told his patient. "Now, put out your tongue."

While the patient sat there with his mouth agape, the doctor wrote out two prescriptions.

"Ah yes," said the doctor, "that's fine, you may shut your mouth," and he gave him the prescriptions and showed him to the door.

"What was that about?" asked his nurse, who was new on the job. "You didn't even look at his mouth, let alone examine his tongue or tonsils."

"No, but it's nice to have a little peace and quiet when I'm writing out prescriptions."

Dr Pullman, the society dentist, tried desperately to soothe his richest but most difficult patient, a Mrs Gruber. "Don't shake your arms like a semaphore and make those faces at me," he begged. "I haven't even started drilling yet."

"I know you haven't," said Mrs Gruber, "but you're standing on my corns."

"Take it from me," the psychologist explained. "The best way to quiet a hysterical girl is to give her a kiss."

"Ah, but how do you get them hysterical?" asked the student.

The maternity ward waiting-room was thick with cigarette smoke and littered with old teacups. Two fathers-to-be were pacing its length in frowning expectancy. Suddenly, one started grumbling.

"Talk about luck," he said. "This has to happen on my holiday!"

"You're complaining!" said the other. "This is our honeymoon!"

In the middle of her psychiatric session, Mrs Blossom suddenly exclaimed, "Doctor, I simply can't resist you! How about a little kiss?"

"Absolutely not!" the doctor replied indignantly. "That would be contrary to the ethics of my profession. Now continue what you were telling me."

"Well, as I was saying," the patient reluctantly resumed, "I'm always having arguments with my husband about his father, and just yesterday — I'm sorry doctor, I just can't go on talking. I have this overwhelming impulse. Come on, what harm would there be if you gave me just one little kiss?"

"That's absolutely impossible!" the doctor snapped. "In fact, I shouldn't even be lying here on this couch with you!"

A somewhat worried woman finally admitted to her doctor what was troubling her.

"It's flatulence, doctor," she blushingly confided. Then, more confident, she continued, "Thank goodness it's silent and odourless, but I'm embarrassed because my dresses billow so obviously at the back. Like that, see!"

The doctor retreated behind his desk and hastily wrote a prescription.

"Take these tablets and come back in ten days," he said.

Ten days later the lady returned, looking somewhat distraught.

"Oh, doctor," she wailed, "since I started taking the tablets the flatulence has started to smell horribly."

"Good news," replied the doctor. "Now that we've fixed your nose we'll make a start on your ears."

What do you get for a man who has everything? Penicillin.

"Doctor, I feel terrible," the conservative business executive moaned. "What's wrong with me?"

"Well, just answer a few questions first," the doctor said. "Do you drink much alcohol?"

"I never touch a drop."

"Do you smoke?" the doctor continued.

"No, tobacco's a filthy weed," the businessman replied indignantly.

"Do you spend many late nights socialising?"

"Of course not!" the patient retorted. "I'm in bed every night by ten-thirty — early to bed and early to rise, that's my motto."

"Well, then, are you experiencing sharp pains in the head?"

"Yes, yes, I suffer from them all the time."

"Just what I thought," the doctor smirked. "Your halo is on too tight!"

"It's dropsy," the doctor explained to the old British brigadier. "There's too much water in the body."

"Never touched a drop of the bloody stuff in my life," the old soldier expostulated. Then, after a moment's reflection, he added, "Must have been all that blasted ice."

Physician: "Well, Mr Stern, you know nobody lives forever."
Patient: "Doctor, do you mind if I try?"

Old Doc Smith passed away and his colleagues decided to take up a collection to pay for his funeral.

They were still short of funds when they approached an eccentric old man who had been a patient of Doc's for many years.

"How much would ya like me to give?" the old fellow mumbled.

"Fifty dollars, to bury the doctor," replied the doctor's representative tentatively.

"*Fifty* dollars?" queried the old man. "Why, take three hundred and bury six of them!"

Agoraphobia ... don't leave home without it.

The poor tailor was beside himself. His wife was sick and perhaps dying. He called on the only doctor nearby.

"Please, save my wife, doctor! I'll pay anything!"

"But what if I can't cure her?" asked the doctor.

"I'll pay whether you cure her or kill her, if only you'll come right away!"

So the doctor promptly visited the woman, but within a week, she died. Soon a bill arrived charging the tailor a tremendous fee. The tailor couldn't hope to pay, so he asked the doctor to appear with him before the local rabbi to arbitrate the case.

"He agreed to pay me for treating his wife," stated the physician, "whether I cured her or killed her."

The rabbi was thoughtful. "Well, did you cure her?" he asked.

"No," admitted the doctor.

"And did you kill her?"

"I certainly did not!" expostulated the physician.

"In that case," the rabbi said with finality, "you have no grounds on which to base a fee."

A man who was suffering from a very bad boil went to the doctor. The doctor took a look at the boil and said to his nurse, "Hand me the poker from the fireplace."

She did, and the doctor thrust it into the fire until it was red hot. Then he jabbed it into the boil. The patient leaped with pain.

"Ah, well," said the doctor, "I'm not much on boils, but one thing I know is how to treat a burn."

"Roll up! Roll up!" said the medicine man at the Easter Fair. "My magical Elixir of Life, distilled from an ancient Egyptian formula, known only to the ancient order of the Priests of Ra until I personally deciphered it from the Dead Sea Scrolls, will positively cure everything from bunions to rigor mortis! Look at me for the living proof, ladies and gentlemen! I am no less than 135 years of age! Hurry, hurry, hurry! While stocks last!"

"Is that true? Is he really 135 years old?" a man in the crowd said to the medicine man's pretty assistant.

"I dunno, mister," she replied, "I've only been working for him for seventy years."

The doctor groaned inwardly as he observed the crotchety old patient entering his surgery, but he put on a brave smile and welcomed him into the room.

"What seems to be the problem, Mr Johnson?" he enquired encouragingly.

"What seems to be the problem? Really, some doctor you are — that's what you're supposed to find out!" The patient launched into his tirade. "Why do you just stand there asking questions? You should work for your money, conduct an examination, consult, before making a diagnosis."

The long-suffering doctor finally cracked.

"Certainly, how silly of me," he snapped. "Just step outside for a moment and wait while I call in a specialist. He should only take an hour or so to arrive — you see he lives out of town, but he's the only doctor I know who can make a medical diagnosis without asking questions — he's a vet!"

The inexperienced intern was thrilled to be able to accompany the celebrated surgeon on his daily hospital rounds. He answered enthusiastically whenever his opinion was asked; undaunted by the fact that his diagnoses were consistently wrong.

In desperation, the surgeon took him aside one morning and gave him some paternal advice: "Have you ever considered becoming an economist?"

Poor Mrs Sanowitz! Her son had been feeling depressed, so he'd gone to see a psychiatrist. And the doctor had told Walter that he had an Oedipus complex!

"What shall I do?" asked the saddened mother to her husband.

Mr Sanowitz was unsympathetic.

"Oedipus-Shmoedipus!" he said disdainfully. "So long as he loves his mother!"

William Dellano Petrie was convinced he was a cannibal. His wife finally persuaded him to visit a psychiatrist.

When Petrie returned home after his first visit, his wife asked, "So tell me, what is a fancy psychiatrist like?"

"Delicious," beamed Petrie.

The nurse was holding the patient by both wrists when the doctor entered the room.

"You don't have to hold both wrists to check the pulse," said the doctor.

"Doctor," she replied, "I'm holding them to check his impulses."

A patient says to his doctor, "My foot hurts, what will I do for it?"

"Limp."

Mr Bellamy was sent by his G.P. to a specialist. Dr Murray examined him thoroughly and told him to get dressed and come into his office.

"Bellamy, I'm afraid I have very bad news for you. You are suffering from extreme leukaemia."

"Oh, my God, doc! Is there any cure?"

"Well, we can try to treat it, but the prospects don't look good."

Completely crushed, Mr Bellamy asked meekly, "How long would you say I have to live?"

"Well, I'm sorry to say . . . about three months."

"Oh, my God! Listen, doc, I'm a relatively young man. I have three young children to support. I just bought a house and am paying off the mortgage and a mountain of bills. In fact, I wouldn't even be able to pay your bills for at least six months."

"In that case," advised Dr Murray, "I'll give you six months to live."

Mrs Bromley called the doctor's office and said to the receptionist, "Listen, did I leave my panties in your office when I was there this morning?"

"Just a second, I'll have someone check the dressing-room."

She was back in a few moments and said, "I'm sorry, Mrs Bromley, we haven't found any panties here."

"Oh, that's all right," said Mrs Bromley. "Then I must have left them in the dentist's office."

A distraught mother came to Dr Robert X. Fields, noted psychiatrist, and disclosed that she was worried to death about her son.

"He goes around all day long emptying ashtrays."

"Well," answered Dr Fields, "that's not so bad. That's a common compulsion of teenagers who are obsessive about neatness and cleanliness. He empties ashtrays. So what?"

"Yes," said Mrs Thomas. "But in his mouth?"

The Brownlock family were despairing. Father Brownlock hadn't been able to sleep for a week and he was getting more and more cantankerous by the minute. They'd tried hot toddies and cold toddies, sleeping draughts and sleeping pills. They'd played lullabies and they'd read him monotonous stories. They'd yawned incessantly at him and snored suggestively in his ear. All to no avail.

"There's only one thing for it," cried Sam Brownlock in haggard desperation, and he called in a renowned hypnotist.

The Great Mesmo fixed Brownlock senior with an impelling eye and began in low, slow tones, "You are going to sleep, deep, deep sleep. As you hear my voice you'll feel drowsier and drowsier until finally you are in a sleep peaceful and deep. The shadows are closing about you and now you are in a deep, deep sleep."

Those of the family who had managed to witness the therapy and themselves remain awake exclaimed in delight at the miracle — Father was asleep. The Great Mesmo was paid handsomely and departed with a flourish.

As the front door closed, Father Brownlock opened one cautious eye.

"That lunatic gone yet?" he demanded.

Specialisation in medicine has gone too far, in the opinion of some of the older physicians. One of them was talking to a medical student who was soon to graduate. "I suppose," said the older man, "that you are going to be a specialist like so many of the young men nowadays?"

"Yes, doctor," said the other. "I am going to specialise in diseases of the nose."

"Indeed?" the older doctor snorted. "Which nostril?"

Well into his twelfth tankard of rum the befuddled bar prop suddenly pitched forward, and his glass eye popped out and into his half-filled tankard.

Unaware of his loss he tossed off his twelfth lot and tottered off.

It was severe constipation that took him to the doctor's the next day.

"Well, I'll have to examine you," said the doctor. "Now take off your trousers and underpants and bend over."

Torch in hand, the doctor was peering into the dark recesses when suddenly he drew back, offended.

"What's the matter!" he cried. "Don't you trust me?"

"What's the verdict, doctor?" asked the nervous patient.

"Well, Mr Jobbins, I think it is malignant and Dr White thinks it is benign, but he'll find out I'm right at the autopsy!"

Clara wasn't feeling well, and she knew she should see a doctor. So she asked her friend Betty for the name of the doctor she used.

"His name's Dunhill," said Betty, "but you should know he's expensive."

"How expensive?" asked Clara.

"Well, it's fifty dollars for the first visit, and twenty-five for every visit after that."

So Clara went off to see Dr Dunhill. When her turn came to be examined, she smiled brightly and said to the nurse, "Hi, honey. Here I am again!"

Dr Dunhill wasn't fooled. After he examined her he said, "O.K., continue the treatment I prescribed on your last visit."

A temperance lecturer produced a large fat worm from a tin and dropped it into a pitcher of whisky. The worm swam round three times at breakneck speed, thrust its head despairingly out of the liquor, gave a last gasp and sank to the bottom — dead.

"There, my friends!" the temperance enthusiast addressed his audience, "and what does that prove?"

At which a rather slurred voice was heard from the rear of the hall. "If you got worms," it called, "drink whisky!"

The doctor was reassuring his patient, "You're going to live until you're sixty."

"I am sixty."

"What did I tell you?"

A lovely but rather flat-chested young woman visited a physician for her periodic physical examination.

"Please remove your blouse," the doctor told her.

"Oh, no," the young lady protested, "I just couldn't!"

"Come, come," the doctor replied, "let's not make mountains out of molehills."

"How can I manage to reawaken my wife's interest in lovemaking?" the man asked his doctor in some desperation. "It's now so bad that it just seems like a monotonous routine."

"Well, I always advise my patients in similar circumstances to try surprise tactics. That usually works."

"You'd better explain, doc."

"Well, for example, when you go home tonight take a dozen red roses and a bottle of champagne. Embrace your wife, nibble on her ear and then carry her off to the bedroom. See if that makes any difference."

The next day, there at the beginning of the waiting-room queue, the ardent spouse sat with a very glum face.

"It didn't work, doc," he explained. "I bought the roses and a magnum of champagne and instead of going back to the office I went straight home. I didn't even wait to open the door, but tore it off its hinges. I grabbed the missus, bit both her ears and, rather than waste time carrying her to the bedroom, I threw her down on the living-room floor and had her right there and then. Made no difference though. It was still the same old monotonous routine ... Mind you, her bridge club got quite a thrill out of it."

Two eminent psychiatrists, one forty years old, the other over seventy, occupied offices in the same building. At the end of a long day, they rode down in the elevator together. The younger man appeared completely done in, and he noted that his senior was still quite fresh.

"I don't understand," said the younger, "how you can listen to patients from morning to night and still look so spry."

The old psychiatrist shrugged his shoulders and replied, "Who listens?"

Joe: "What's Dr Poe's specialty?"
Moe: "Oh, he diagnoses wallets."

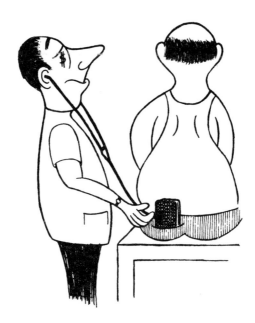

"What's to be done, doc?" the Aussie stockman asked. "I haven't been to the dunny for a bloody week."

"It's constipation, son. No worries, we'll have you active in no time," reassured the doctor. "Now these here pills I'm prescribing I want you to insert, one a day, in the rectum."

"Eh?" said the stockman, scratching his head.

"The back passage, mate," explained the doctor.

A week later the doctor ran into his patient again.

"You look terrible," he said. "Didn't the tablets work?"

"Listen, doc, I tried putting those bloody tablets in the back passage, no good. So I thought I'd try the front hall. No good. Tried them in the kitchen, and on the verandah. For all the bloody good they did I might as well have stuck them up me bloody arse!"

Bill Jones sat patiently in his doctor's surgery while a deep wound on his forehead was being bathed and stitched.

"How did it happen?" asked the doctor.

"It's a long story, doc," Bill said. "But you see, it was like this. Twenty years ago I was a travelling salesman. It was my first job and I was very raw and a true innocent. Well, one night I walked into a little country hotel and saw a beautiful girl registering ahead of me. Later, I found she was given the room next to mine and soon after I went to bed, I heard a knock at the door. When I opened it, sure enough, there she was and in a flimsy nightgown too. She told me she was cold and asked if I could lend her a blanket. I did and she went back to her room. A while later, she returned, said she was freezing and asked if I could lend her a spare set of pyjamas. I did and she left. Well, doc, this morning I was at home mending a broken table. I had a hammer in my hand and I got to thinking about that incident twenty years ago. Suddenly, I realised what the girl had really wanted. I slapped my hand to my head, and that's how I cut my forehead."

A mental patient complained so bitterly about severe stomach pains that the doctor finally decided to operate — and inside the poor fellow he found a bouquet of roses.

"Now, how the hell did those flowers get in there?" he exclaimed.

"Damned if I know," said the patient. "Let's look at the card and see who they're from."

"This is ridiculous," the surgeon complained as he collected his car after it had been serviced. "Four hundred and twenty dollars for looking over the engine and grinding some valves? Your charge for labour is far too high!"

"Really?" said the service station owner laconically. "As a surgeon, you of all people should realise that an automobile engine is just as complicated as the human body and requires very delicate handling. The mechanic who worked on your car is just as skilled at his job as you are at yours."

"Well then," said the surgeon, "I'd like to see him grinding valves while the engine is running."

A frantic woman burst through the door and confronted the man sitting behind the desk.

"Doctor, the waiting is killing me! Tell me honestly, what is the matter with me?"

The young man looked her over with a critical eye and said, "Madam, I have three things to tell you. Firstly, you are carrying far too much weight. Secondly, you should remove at least four layers of rouge and foundation and let your skin breathe. And lastly, you're in the wrong office. The doctor's office is next door. I'm an artist."

Felix Simmons was a nice guy, but a social flop. Although he was thirty-five, he had never conquered his childhood habit of bedwetting. Finally, one of his dear friends told him, "Look, Felix, you might as well know the truth. We're all very fond of you, but nobody can stand to come into your house because it smells, and you're driving your wife up the wall. Why don't you see a psychiatrist about your problem? Enuresis is not too uncommon and it can be cured. Get it over with once and for all."

Felix was convinced. After six months of treatment he ran into the same friend. "Well, Felix, did you take my advice?"

"Yes," answered Felix, "I've been seeing a psychiatrist three times a week for four months now."

"Well, have you had any results?"

"Oh," beamed Felix, "great results!"

"You don't wet your bed any more?"

"I still do, but now I'm proud of it."

"My daughter thinks she is a chicken," the mother told the psychiatrist.

"How long has this condition existed?" the doctor wanted to know.

"About six years," the good lady admitted.

"Why did you delay so long before coming to me?" demanded the doctor.

"Well, frankly, we needed the eggs," said the mother.

The aged patient, an outstanding boozer, complained to his doctor of deafness.

"You'll have to give up the drink Patrick, it's the only way," the doctor advised.

Patrick sadly agreed to take the cure.

However, some months later the patient lurched unsteadily into the doctor's office.

"Are you drinking again, Patrick?"

"I sure am, doc."

"But why?"

"Guess I liked what I was drinking more than what I was hearing."

A doctor asked his woman patient, "Do you know what the most effective birth control pill is?"

She replied, "No."

"That's it!" he said.

The room was darkened and the ophthalmologist asked the patient to read the top line of a chart. He slowly spelled it out: "ZYKSRYMNZDPZ ... Hey, I know that guy," he said. "He's a Polish migrant living at Greenwich."

The doctor smiled and told the middle-aged matron, "I wouldn't worry about your son playing with dolls."

"I'm not worried," said the woman, "but his wife is very upset."

Josh was in the pub partaking of liquid comfort. His wife was in hospital in a very grave condition.

"I don't know whether she'll live or die," he explained to the barman.

"But surely the doctor gave you an idea of her chances," the barman sympathised.

"Well, he said to prepare for the worst but damned if that hasn't got me guessing."

The pretty young patient entered the dressing-room and started disrobing. "I don't get it," she exclaimed to another patient who was sitting there, completely nude, holding a black bag on her lap, "I tell the doctor I'm here because my sinus is bothering me and he tells me to strip!"

"That's nothing," replied the nude. "I just came here to tune the piano!"

A man consulted a psychiatrist for help with various problems. The analyst said, "Stretch out here on the couch. Just relax and tell me about your early life. Just keep on talking. Say anything that comes to mind."

The man proceeded to spill out his life's story. Suddenly the analyst took out a big balloon and, sitting behind the patient, blew it up to full size. Then he stuck a pin in it. The balloon burst with a loud crash. The patient was startled. The doctor said sharply, "Now tell me, quick, what did you think about when you heard the loud explosion?"

"I thought of sex."

"Sex? At such a moment? You thought about sex?"

"Well," said the patient, "what's so surprising about that? It's all I ever think about."

M ax Wellington went to his doctor for a checkup. After the examination, Dr Newton told him, "Max, you're in wonderful condition for a man of seventy. You should live to be one hundred!"

"Oh, thank you, doctor. Listen, will you please do a blood test on me? I'm getting married in a week."

"How wonderful, Max! Congratulations! And who is the lucky woman?"

"Well, I don't know if you know her. She's Laura Baxter. She lives in my street."

"Of course I know Laura. She's a patient of mine, too. But, listen Max, if you're marrying Laura there's something you should know about her. She's got acute angina."

"You're telling me, doc!"

M y wife's at death's door!"
"Don't worry. I'll pull her through."

"I'm afraid I've adopted a terrible habit," the patient told his psychiatrist. "Wherever I am, I can't help talking to myself. Is there anything you can do for me?"

"I suppose there is," the psychiatrist replied. "But I should warn you it will be a long, slow, painful treatment, and very expensive as well. But suppose you do talk to yourself. Is that so bad?"

"No, I guess it isn't," the patient agreed. "But I'm *such* a bore."

A group of Peace Corps volunteers were being briefed before leaving for a remote African country.

"Now, boys," the doctor told them, "you may very well run across some poisonous snakes where you're going, and one of you could be bitten. Let me say, first of all, that no matter what you've heard, drinking whisky is no antidote. If you're bitten by a snake, you must make a cut near the bite so that it bleeds freely. Then put your mouth over the gash, and suck out as much blood as you can."

"But, sir," one recruit called out, "suppose you're bitten on the behind?"

The doctor stared back and cracked a grin. "Then, my boy, you'll find out who your friends are."

V irus: A Latin word meaning your guess is as good as mine.

Mrs Moskowitz was ageing. She had passed eighty-one and was having some "woman trouble". Upon the advice of her daughter, she went to visit a gynaecologist. She remained quiet throughout the examination, but when it was over she turned to Dr Lipsky.

"Dr Lipsky," she said, "you seem to be such a nice young man. Tell me, does your mother know how you're making a living?"

The lady told the psychiatrist, "My husband thinks I'm crazy just because I like pancakes."

"But there's nothing wrong with that," said the doctor. "I like pancakes myself."

"Do you?" cried the lady in delight. "Then you must come up some time. I have six trunks full."

A vasectomy means never having to say you're sorry.

A quack is a medical term for a competitor.

As the doctor was on his daily round through the men's surgical ward, he heard a howl of pain from behind a curtained bed. He pulled back the curtains to investigate.

"But nurse," he cried, "I said prick his boil . . ."

Doctor: "Well, you'll get along O.K. Your left leg is swollen but I wouldn't worry about it."
Patient: "No, and if your left leg was swollen, I wouldn't worry about it, either."

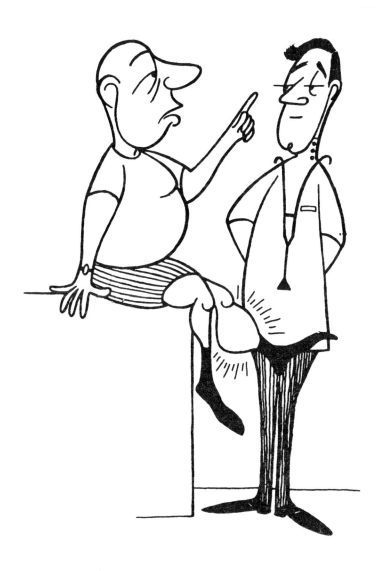

Patient: "Doc, how long can a person live after his brain stops functioning?"
Doc: "I don't know. How old are you?"

Mary and Jeanette were making their once-a-month telephone call for keeping up-to-date on each other's gossip.

"Oh, and Mary," said Jeanette, "did I tell you the latest about my son David?"

"No, what about David?" asked Mary.

"He is going to a psychiatrist!" said his mother proudly. "Twice a week he goes to a psychiatrist!"

Mary knew she was supposed to be impressed, but she didn't really understand why. "Is that good?" she asked.

"Of course it's good!" exclaimed Jeanette. "Imagine, fifty dollars an hour he pays, fifty dollars! And all he talks about is me!"

Dr Goldman's patients kept calling him up night and day.

One Friday afternoon he said to his wife, "Listen, I'm absolutely worn out, Louise. I need a real rest. I want to stay home and have some peace and quiet. Just tell my patients I'm out of town at a medical meeting."

Sure enough, at one o'clock that morning the phone rang. Mrs Goldman answered it and told the caller that Dr Goldman was out of town.

"But, Mrs Goldman, I have a six-month-old infant who's crying all night long, and I don't know what to do."

"Just a minute." Covering up the mouthpiece, she told her husband that Mrs Kramer wanted to know what to do about her sick infant.

"Tell her to give the baby formula."

"Mrs Kramer," said Mrs Goldman into the phone, "give your baby formula."

"Oh, thank you. But how often?"

"Just a minute, Mrs Kramer."

Again Mrs Goldman asked Dr Goldman how often Mrs Kramer should give her baby formula.

"Tell her every four hours."

"Every four hours," Mrs Goldman advised Mrs Kramer.

"Oh, thank you so much," said Mrs Kramer gratefully. "But I have just one more question to ask you. Is that guy you're in bed with also a doctor?"

Mr Andrews, a young man of twenty-eight, went to see his doctor and told him he wanted to be castrated.

"But my dear Mr Andrews," exclaimed the doctor, "why on earth would a healthy young man like you want to take such a drastic step?"

"Please, Dr Barley, do not try to dissuade me. I've given it a lot of thought and I'm sure that that's what I want."

"Well, if you insist," said Dr Barley, shaking his head in complete befuddlement, "all right."

The operation was scheduled and completed, and Mr Andrews was wheeled back into his room.

The next day, Mr Andrews felt much better and started chatting with his room-mate, as hospital patients do.

"And what puts you in the hospital?" Mr Andrews asked.

"Oh, I decided to be circumcised," replied his neighbour.

"Oh my God!" shrieked Mr Andrews, clutching his head, "*that's* the word I meant."

The sink in the doctor's office was leaking badly and the plumber was called. He took the whole thing apart and after about an hour he put it all together again, and it was working properly. The plumber then wrote out a bill for $200.

The doctor took a look at the bill and shrieked. "My God, you were here less than an hour. I'm a doctor and I don't get $200 an hour!"

"I know," said the plumber calmly. "When I was a doctor, I didn't either."